MEXICO
Leading the Southern Hemisphere

FAMOUS PEOPLE
OF MEXICAN HISTORY

The region that today is called Mexico has produced some of the most interesting figures in Western history.

MEXICO
Leading the Southern Hemisphere

FAMOUS PEOPLE OF MEXICAN HISTORY

MC MASON CREST
PHILADELPHIA

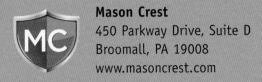

Mason Crest
450 Parkway Drive, Suite D
Broomall, PA 19008
www.masoncrest.com

©2015 by Mason Crest, an imprint of National Highlights, Inc.

Printed and bound in the United States of America.

CPSIA Compliance Information: Batch #M2014.
For further information, contact Mason Crest at 1-866-MCP-Book.

First printing

1 3 5 7 9 8 6 4 2

Library of Congress Cataloging-in-Publication Data
        on file at the Library of Congress

        ISBN: 978-1-4222-3215-6 (hc)
        ISBN: 978-1-4222-8680-7 (ebook)

Mexico: Leading the Southern Hemisphere series ISBN: 978-1-4222-3213-2

TABLE OF CONTENTS

MEXICO
Leading the Southern Hemisphere

KEY ICONS TO LOOK FOR:

 Text-dependent questions: These questions send the reader back to the text for more careful attention to the evidence presented there.

 Words to understand: These words with their easy-to-understand definitions will increase the reader's understanding of the text, while building vocabulary skills.

 Series glossary of key terms: This back-of-the book glossary contains terminology used throughout this series. Words found here increase the reader's ability to read and comprehend higher-level books and articles in this field.

 Research projects: Readers are pointed toward areas of further inquiry connected to each chapter. Suggestions are provided for projects that encourage deeper research and analysis.

 Sidebars: This boxed material within the main text allows readers to build knowledge, gain insights, explore possibilities, and broaden their perspectives by weaving together additional information to provide realistic and holistic perspectives.

TIMELINE

12th century	Topiltzin rules the Toltecs.
1325	The city of Tenochtitlán is built.
1427-1440	Under Itzcoatl, the Aztecs expand their empire.
1440-1468	Under Montezuma I, the Aztecs' power grows still greater.
1502	Montezuma II becomes emperor of the Aztecs.
1519	Cortés arrives in Mexico and begins his conquest.
1810	Miguel Hidalgo y Castilla begins the War of Independence against Spain.
1821	Agustín de Iturbide successfully leads Mexican forces to Independence against Spain.
1822-1823	Agustín de Iturbide is "Emperor of Mexico."
1833	Santa Anna becomes president for the first of 11 times.
1846-1848	War between Mexico and the United States, in which Mexico is defeated and loses half its territory to the United States.
1855	Santa Anna is overthrown by liberal forces.
1857	Mexico has a new and liberal constitution.
1858-1861	The War of Reform is fought between conservative forces and liberal forces, led by Benito Juárez.
1864	Maximilian, Archduke of Austria, is crowned Emperor of Mexico.
1867	Liberal armies defeat the Empire, and Juárez returns to power.
1877	Porfirio Díaz seizes power and controls the presidency for 34 years.

1910-1911 Francisco Madero leads the Revolution and overthrows the government of Diaz.

1934-1940 Lázaro Cárdenas is president of the Republic.

1968 Student Movement ends when the army fires on the crowd in Tlatelolco; Agustín Yáñez, secretary of education, works to prevent further violence.

1994 In the southern state of Chiápas, an armed revolt causes the worst political and economic crisis in modern Mexico's history.

2000 Vicente Fox, the candidate for the conservative National Action Party, is elected president.

2001 President Fox meets with U.S. President George W. Bush to discuss a cooperative relationship between the neighboring countries.

2002 Latin American leaders, including Mexico's Vicente Fox, meet in Argentina for the Global Alumni Conference to discuss technological and economic issues.

2006 Felipe Calderón is sworn in as Mexico's president in December.

2007 The Museum of the Fine Arts in Mexico City honors the 100th birthday of Frida Kahlo with the first comprehensive exhibit of her paintings in Mexico. Open from mid-June through mid-August, the exhibit draws record crowds.

2012 Josefina Vázquez Mota, the first woman to run for president of Mexico as candidate of a major party, is defeated by Enrique Peña Nieto.

WORDS TO UNDERSTAND

aqueduct—a structure for carrying flowing water.

bureaucracy—a system of government administration made up of nonelected officers.

conquistadors—the Spanish conquerors of the New World.

A statue of Montezuma II, one of the greatest rulers of ancient Mexico. As the ninth emperor of the Aztecs from 1502 until 1519, he created laws that pulled the empire together. It was his misfortune to be on the throne when Spanish soldiers under Hernán Cortés arrived.

ANCIENT LEADERS

Before the Spanish *conquistadors* set foot on the shores of Mexico, tribes of diverse native people had flourished there, including the Olmecs, the Toltecs, the Maya, and the Aztecs. The records that their sophisticated civilizations left behind tell of the accomplishments of great tribal leaders.

One such leader was Topiltzin Acxitl Quetzalcoatl, a 12th-century Toltec chieftain. Topiltzin was one of the last leaders of the powerful Toltec empire, which collapsed in the 12th century. The Aztecs, who thought of the Toltecs as their ancestors, revered Topiltzin as a god, and they kept his story alive.

Topiltzin's father was the ruler of the Toltec tribe, but he was assassinated when Topiltzin was a young man. Topiltzin avenged the murder and retook the throne, becoming the ruler of the Toltecs. He eliminated his enemies and focused his power in the city of Tula, the center of the Toltec empire.

Topiltzin was devoted to his belief in the peaceful god of knowledge, Quetzalcoatl. Eventually, he took on the name Quetzalcoatl, and the Aztecs believed he also assumed the powers of this kindly god.

However, Topiltzin Quetzalcoatl's kingdom was not peaceful. The forces that had led to his father's assassination continued to oppose him. Also, other tribes at the borders of the kingdom fought against his people. Because of this fighting, Topiltzin Quetzalcoatl was driven from his throne, never to return.

The Aztecs believed that Topiltzin Queztalcoatl disappeared in the east. In some versions of the story, he died but later appeared in the heavens as Venus, the morning star.

The Aztecs admired Topiltzin Queztalcoatl for his ability to control his kingdom through his wisdom and strength. These qualities were important to the Aztecs. Aztec records show that Itzcoatl, ruler of the Aztecs from 1427 to 1440, shared these qualities.

The Aztecs were a tribe of warriors who came from the north and settled in central Mexico, and Itzcoatl was an early founder of their empire. Because other tribes occupied much of the same territory, the Aztecs were forced to live on land no one else wanted, on a swampy island in the middle of Lake Texcoco. They claimed as their own the ancient city of Tenochtitlán, which was first settled in 1325.

During the reign of Itzcoatl, the original Aztec settlement began to be transformed into an amazing city. The Aztecs enlarged the small islands of the lake and created "floating gardens" from mud dredged from the lake bottom. The islands were connected to the shore by stone causeways, which had removable sections for defending the Aztec city.

The Aztecs were able to build Tenochtitlán's new splendor because Itzcoatl's leadership made it possible. He negotiated a treaty, which was called the Triple Alliance, with two other powerful tribes. Because the Aztecs had allies, they spent less time and money fighting off their enemies. Thanks to Itzcoatl's wisdom and diplomacy, the Aztecs had the time and the resources to build their great imperial center in the middle of Lake Texcoco.

13

This native painting on cloth gives an idea of the size of Tenochtitlán, the Aztec capital. When the Spanish arrived in Mexico, Tenochtitlán was home to about 300,000 people, making it larger than any city of Europe at the time. Although the Aztecs had developed a complex government structure, a powerful military, a state religion, and an artistic tradition, Spanish conquistadors still viewed them as savages.

14

TWO IMPORTANT GODS OF THE TOLTECS AND AZTECS:

Quetzalcoatl was the god of wind, light, and the morning star (Venus). He was also the god of knowledge and the founder of agriculture. Represented as a feathered serpent, he was a kind god, giving humans all the good aspects of civilization, including science, the calendar, and corn. Quetzalcoatl was worshipped by Mexican cultures more ancient than the Aztecs, including the Toltecs and the Mayas. He was considered to be the founder of the Toltec civilization. Sometimes Quetzalcoatl was depicted as a white man with a black beard. That's one of the reasons why Montezuma II believed that Cortés might have been Quetzalcoatl returning from the east.

The Aztecs believed the most powerful god was *Huitzilopoctli*, who was the god of the sun and war. In their belief system, Huitzilopoctli struggled with the forces of night to keep humans alive in the on-going battle between night and day. He needed the blood of human sacrifice to give him strength to fight his battle against the forces of night. He was a very important god to the Aztecs, because they believed that it was Huitzilopoctli who showed them where to build the city of Tenochtitlán.

Montezuma I was another great Aztec leader. He ruled from 1440 to 1468. Because he established the structure of the Aztec empire, he is considered the greatest of the Aztec rulers. During his reign, the city of Tenochtitlán was made even more beautiful and comfortable for its citizens, and his empire grew in size and wealth.

Montezuma I improved the city by having an ***aqueduct*** built, which brought fresh water from the nearby mountains. He was responsible for creating a botanical garden with plants from all over his empire. He also enlarged the great pyramid in the center of the city by adding two temples at the top, one to Tlaloc, the rain god, and one to Huitzilopochtli, the god of war and the sun.

Montezuma I was able to pay for these improvements by sending out his warriors and

AZTEC SERPENT FIGURE.

Quetzalcoatl has been depicted in several forms, such as a feathered serpent (left) or a god emerging from the mouth of the earth (right). One of the most revered gods of the ancient Aztecs, tradition had it that Quetzalcoatl introduced maize, a vital crop to the people.

forcing other tribes to submit to Aztec rule. He expanded the Aztec empire to the Gulf of Mexico to the east and to the Pacific in the south. The tribes that came within the domain of Montezuma I had to pay tribute, a tax for the protection of this powerful empire. From these other tribes in their territories, the Aztecs collected tribute of maize (corn), rubber, feathers, copper, and weapons. Prisoners of war were another kind of tribute that inspired great fear in the tribes, especially since these prisoners were sacrificed to Huitzilopochtli,

A skull sculpture in Templo Mayor, the main temple of the Aztecs at the time of the Spanish arrival. The remains of the temple can still be seen in Mexico City today.

the god of war. A man of great power, Montezuma I shaped an empire of beauty and terror for generations to come.

One of the last great leaders of the Aztecs was a descendant of the first Montezuma, Montezuma II, who ruled the Aztec empire from 1502 to 1520. Like his predecessors, he was not only a ruler but also a warrior and priest. He was called *huey tlatoani*, which means "great king" in the Aztec language.

Montezuma II is remembered for organizing the ***bureaucracy*** of his empire. He established stricter rules about social structure and controlled the outer boundaries of his empire. However, during his reign, the Triple Alliance, established by Itzcoatl, began to break down, so Montezuma II had to control many rebellions in his territories.

Montezuma II is also remembered for being the Aztec ruler who greeted the Spanish conquistador, Hernán Cortés, and his army at the entrance to the city of Tenochtitlán. Montezuma II had hesitated to send his warriors out to destroy

Cortés. There had been omens that indicated to Montezuma that Cortés might be the god Quetzalcoatl, returning from the east. Montezuma II did not want to harm a god, but he did not trust these invaders.

Cortés took advantage of Montezuma's indecision. When Montezuma II invited Cortés and his men to be his guests in the city, Cortés took him hostage in his own palace. In the end, Montezuma II died as a prisoner of the Spanish conquistador, after he was hit in the head by a rock, thrown at him from a crowd of his own people who thought he had betrayed them to the Spanish conquerors. He died three days later, leaving his son, Cuauhtemoc, to lead the losing war against the Spanish.

TEXT-DEPENDENT QUESTIONS

Who ruled the Aztec empire from 1427 to 1440?

What is the name of the lake where Tenochtitlán, the Aztec capital, was located?

RESEARCH PROJECT

Before the arrival of the Spanish in the 16th century, the people of Mesoamerica recorded their history in books called codices. Visit http://www.library.arizona.edu/exhibits/mex-codex/featcdx.htm and click on the links to see examples of Aztec and Mayan codices. Observe how they used images and pictographs to tell their stories.

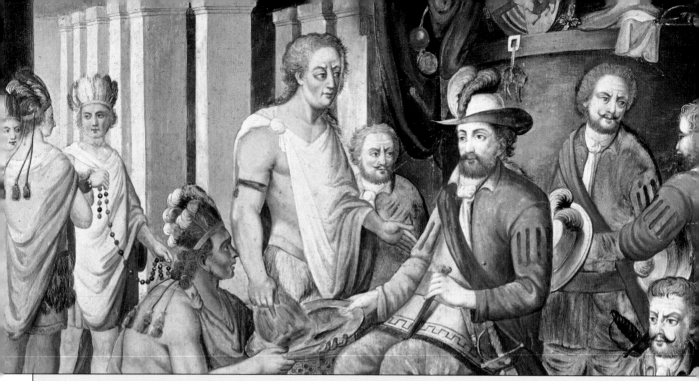

 WORDS TO UNDERSTAND

ambushed—attacked by surprise from a hidden location.

armada—a fleet of Spanish warships.

civil war—a conflict fought between citizens of the same country.

conservative—wanting to maintain things the way they are with no reforms or changes, the opposite of liberal.

democratic—believing that government belongs to the people.

exile—when a person is forced to leave his or her home.

guerrilla—someone who fights using sabotage and surprise tactics.

moderate—sticking to the middle of the road politically (between liberals and conservatives).

CONQUERORS, SOLDIERS, AND REVOLUTIONARIES

The first European to have a great impact on the history of Mexico was Hernán Cortés. Looking back on their history, Mexicans disagree about whether Cortés was a hero or a villain, because he was the Spanish conquistador who overthrew the Aztec empire and won Mexico for the Spanish crown. While some say he brought the advantages of European civilization to Mexico, others say he is responsible for the near-destruction of Mexico's native civilizations.

Hernán Cortés was an aristocrat from Extremadura, a province in Spain that produced many other conquistadors. Although he originally went to Española, then Cuba, he was given command of an ***armada*** to explore the mainland. When he landed in Yucatán, he found a shipwrecked Spaniard who spoke Mayan, the language of the tribe who lived there. This tribe gave him La Malinche (also called Doña Marina), a native woman who could speak both Mayan and the language of the Aztecs.

With their help as interpreters, Cortés moved inland, fighting and negotiating with the tribes he encountered. When he reached the Aztec city of

20

Tenochtitlán, Montezuma II welcomed him. However, Cortés soon forced Montezuma II to acknowledge the Spanish king as his overlord.

After subduing the Aztec people of Tenochtitlán, Cortés destroyed the Aztec temples. The bloody rituals of human sacrifice shocked him, and he wanted to replace Aztec beliefs with Christianity. This angered the Aztecs. After Montezuma's death, his son Cuauhtemoc led his people's resistance against Cortés and his soldiers, but the superior weapons of the Spanish overpowered the Aztec warriors.

In colonial Mexico, the Roman Catholic church was a powerful institution. Spanish rulers generally constructed a church at the center of every town, and worked to convert the people to their religion. This cathedral is located in Merida, on the Yucatan peninsula. It was built on top of a Mayan religious shrine, and completed in 1598.

From the center of the Aztec empire, Cortés sent troops north, south, east, and west in order to subdue the rest of the country. However, conquering and controlling Mexico became the work of other representatives of the Spanish king, as Cortés was eventually sent back to Spain.

In spite of his accomplishments as a conquistador, Cortés did not end his life as a hero. Instead, he died in Spain, angry and bitter at being forced from the leadership position in New Spain. Although he was a Spaniard, Cortés asked to be buried in Mexico.

In the wake of Cortés, Mexico became a colony of Spain. Many people from Spain settled there in the hopes of making their fortune, and Mexico supplied Spain with the riches of its natural resources. For nearly 300 years, Spain controlled Mexico. In fact, no one born in Mexico could be part of its own government. Only men born in Spain could rule Mexico.

But in the 18th century, many people in Mexico felt it was time to rule themselves. Mexicans of European descent (called *criollos*), as well as those of mixed Indian and European descent (called *mestizos*) began to push for Mexican independence from Spain. One of these men was a landowner named Agustín de Iturbide.

At first, Iturbide was not on the side of independence. He was the son of a wealthy Spanish landowner and a Mexican mother. He became a soldier at age 17, first fighting against the rebels who

 Iturbide was at his best as a warrior. In his memoirs, he wrote about how he felt about being in battle:

I was always happy during the war, victory was the inseparable companion of the troops I commanded. I did not lose one battle; I defeated as many enemy troops as attacked me or I encountered, even when they outnumbered me, as they often did, by ten to one.

The Plan of Iguala, a new system of government for Mexico, was the brainchild of Agustín de Iturbide. Iturbide soon became dictator of the country; this Mexican print shows him riding into Mexico City in triumph. However, he would rule Mexico for only a short period, until his repressive measures led to a revolt by Santa Anna. He was exiled in 1823; when he returned a year later, he was executed.

wanted Mexican independence, including Miguel Hidalgo (who is discussed in a later chapter). After losing favor with the Royalists, who supported Spain, he retired. Worried about changes in Spanish politics that could affect Mexico, he later joined forces with the rebels, who wanted Mexico to be a modern *democratic* nation.

With his former enemies, he came up with the Plan de Iguala (1821), a plan for a new government in Mexico. This plan had three important ideas: independence from Spain, Catholicism as the state religion, and equality of all races, including Indians, mestizos, and criollos. But when the Independence forces won under Iturbide's leadership, they disagreed about how to form a new government.

In the confusion of 1822, Iturbide was proclaimed "Emperor of Mexico" by *conservative* military forces. Unfortunately, Iturbide was a better soldier than politician. Even though the economy was ruined by the war, he wanted to rule with the style and luxury of a king, ignoring the democratic goals of his former allies. By end of the year, he had broken up the new congress and proclaimed himself dictator. Rebel forces soon overwhelmed him. In 1823, he stepped down and left Mexico.

Antonio López de Santa Anna was leader of Mexico on 11 different occasions. He was considered a brave military leader but a ruthless politician.

24

 In the United States, Santa Anna is remembered for his role in the history of Texas. In 1835, his soldiers marched on an American colony in Texas, which was then part of Mexico. These settlers had rebelled against Mexican authority, even though they had agreed to abide by Mexican laws when they asked to colonize this northern part of Mexico. Santa Anna's forces killed all 183 defenders of the fort at the Alamo. Revenge for this loss motivated Texan soldiers, who cried, "Remember the Alamo" during the battle of San Jacinto six weeks later, at which Texas won its freedom.

Because Iturbide felt that Mexico needed him, he returned from *exile* in Europe in 1824 to reclaim the throne. Soon after arriving on Mexico's shore, he was executed by those who had opposed his dictatorship.

The man who led the forces that defeated Iturbide was Antonio López de Santa Anna. As an army officer and statesman, he was leader of Mexico between 1833 and 1855, 11 different times. He was considered a brave military leader and a wily politician, a courageous hero and a power-hungry villain.

Santa Anna's abilities as a military leader were important in the turbulent years that followed the Mexican War of Independence. Because Mexico had borrowed money from other countries to fight its war, it had many debts to pay afterward. It could not repay those debts easily because so much of the country had been destroyed in the fighting. But France and the United States, who had loaned Mexico money, were determined to have the money repaid. Led by Santa Anna, Mexico went to war with France and then the United States because of these debts.

Santa Anna used his military success to gain political power. After successfully driving French forces out, he became dictator of Mexico. He lost his position and was exiled to Cuba, but he returned to fight against American forces in the Mexican-American War of 1846. Many Mexicans still blame Santa

Revolutionary leader Emiliano Zapata (1879-1919) is seated in the center of this photo, taken in 1911. He is surrounded by his military advisors, including his brother Eufemio Zapata, who is seated on the left.

Anna for losing this war and negotiating away half Mexico's territories to the United States.

In spite of this failure, Santa Anna returned to power several more times. His last chance at running the country came in 1853, when the Mexican congress's conservative leaders asked him to be king of Mexico. He was soon overthrown by liberal forces and went into final exile in 1855.

At the beginning of the 20th century, Mexico was ready for another revolution, this time a revolution whose goals were to create a more democratic society. One of the best-known warriors of the Revolution was Emiliano Zapata.

He was a passionate leader of Indian descent from the southern state of Morelos.

He organized the Indian and mestizo people in the south to fight for a chance to farm their own land instead of working for the rich landowners. His motto was "Tierra y Libertad" (Land and Freedom). He led guerrilla troops in the south during the years of the revolution, but military victory was not enough; he wanted reform.

At first, Zapata's troops, called *zapatistas*, fought alongside the most powerful group of revolutionary forces. When this **moderate** group finally seized power, Zapata decided to fight against them, too. After meeting with their leader, Francisco Madero, Zapata realized that land reform was not a priority of the new government.

In spite of the chaotic situation in Mexico during the years of the Revolution, Zapata controlled his home state. In Morelos, Zapata put his program for land reform, called the Plan de Ayala, into effect. His followers could put down their weapons and take up their tools for farming. Unfortunately, he never lived to see the rewards of his leadership. Zapata was **ambushed** by government soldiers and killed in 1919.

Traditional wars were fought by well-armed soldiers, who faced each other on battlefields. Zapata could not fight this way because his soldiers did not have weapons as powerful as those of the government's armies. So he became a *guerrilla*, fighting in surprise attacks, often at night and with small groups of soldiers.

Like Emiliano Zapata, Pancho Villa was a guerrilla leader of the Mexican Revolution, but he fought in the northern state of Chihuahua. Unlike Zapata, Villa had been on the wrong side of the law before the Revolution, having joined a gang of bandits when he was 17. Although Villa had settled down, married, and

Pancho Villa (1878–1923) was a sort of Mexican Robin Hood—some people considered him a hero, while others viewed him as a dangerous bandit

opened a butcher's shop, he picked up his guns once again in 1910. He decided to become a soldier for the landowners who supported the revolution.

In the 10 years of *civil war*, he used what he had learned as a bandit to become a military strategist and a leader of the revolutionary armies of northern Mexico. Because he had conflicts with Victoriano Huerta, the commander-in-chief of the republican forces, he was imprisoned in 1912, but he escaped to Texas.

After the old government fell and the new government took over, Villa met with Zapata. They agreed to keep fighting the new government. They didn't believe that the new government would be much better than the old one for people like them, who never had much money or power. Unlike Zapata, Villa survived the Revolution and retired. He was killed by his enemies in 1923.

TEXT-DEPENDENT QUESTIONS

What is the difference between a *criollo* and a *mestizo*?

What Mexican leader ruled the country in 11 different periods during the 19th century?

RESEARCH PROJECT

In 1916, Pancho Villa's men crossed the border into the United states and attacked the town of Columbus, New Mexico, killing 19 people. In response, the United States government sent troops into Mexico to capture Villa. Find out more about Villa's raid, and write a report that explains why the Mexican leader crossed the border. Explain whether what Villa did was justified, using examples that support your position.

WORDS TO UNDERSTAND

civilian—a member of society who does not belong to the military, the police, or the fire department.

liberal—believing in progress and the protection of human rights, the opposite of conservative.

peasants—common people.

progressive—believing in political change and social improvement through government action.

radical—in favor of taking extreme measures to achieve political goals.

This statue of Father Miguel Hidalgo stands in a village plaza. On the day after Independence Day throughout Mexico, statues of the priest are decorated with flowers to honor his role in winning Mexico's freedom from Spain.

THE POLITICIANS AND SHAPERS OF A NATION

Miguel Hidalgo was a Catholic priest from Spain who is remembered as the father of Mexican independence. He was born to wealthy *criollo* parents in Guanajuato, where he studied to be a priest and teacher. Later, he was dismissed from his teaching post because of his **liberal** ideas and behavior. But he was beloved by the Indians who were his parishioners in the village of Dolores.

In the years before the War of Independence, Hidalgo became the leader of a literary club that did more than read books. They plotted for Mexican independence. When their plot was discovered, Hidalgo decided to begin his revolution, even though he was not prepared. The fight for Mexican independence began in 1810 when Hidalgo issued the *Grito de Dolores* (Cry of Dolores), which demanded freedom for all Mexicans and an end to bad government.

Hidalgo's message appealed to the lower levels of Mexican society, the **peasants**, workers, and Indians who wanted revenge for social, economic, and racial injustice. However, Hidalgo couldn't control the violence of his followers, whose cry was "Death to the *gachupines* (Spanish-born Mexicans)".

The government fought back harshly and successfully. Six months later, Hidalgo was captured and executed. He had led only with ideas. He didn't have a real political or military strategy, other than to rid Mexico of the old order in order to create a new, more just order. Mexico's War of Independence had to wait for other leaders.

One of the most beloved figures in Mexican history is Benito Juárez, a hero and president who fought to establish a democratic government. Juárez was born into a Zapotec Indian family but became an orphan at an early age. Fortunately, a benefactor paid for his education to become a priest. Instead, he studied law and became a politician.

After serving in the state and national legislature, Juárez became governor of his native state of Oaxaca in 1848. However, Santa Anna forced him from Mexico because of his liberal ideas. In 1855, he returned and fought against Santa Anna's regime, eventually becoming minister of justice under a new, more democratic president.

One of his most important acts was to write the *Ley* (law) *Juárez*, which took away power from the rich and powerful Catholic Church and the military and gave legal authority to the ***civilian*** government. He also helped to write the new constitution of Mexico in 1857.

Hidalgo's passion for justice in Mexico can be heard in the words of his last sermon, given to the Indians of Saltillo:

"...I have come from the south, from making war on the Spaniards in order to tear the country out of their hands, for it does not belong to them and they have held it for a long time with cruelty and tyranny and grave damage to the original inhabitants, the children of the nation..."

Born to Zapotec parents in Oaxaca, Benito Pablo Juárez went on to become Mexico's president twice. His birthday is now a national holiday across the country.

Juárez was part of a government that made many changes, too many for some Mexicans. Conservative factions tried to take control of government in the costly War of Reform. Then, they conspired with the French to bring in Archduke Maximilian from Austria to be emperor of Mexico. Forced to leave Mexico again, Juárez continued to lead the liberal government. Its forces resisted and eventually got rid of the foreign emperor.

Because he was considered so just and wise, Juárez was elected president four times. He died in office in 1872. He is remembered as a great leader because he rose to power as an Indian in a prejudiced society and maintained his power as a civilian in a time of military power.

Porfirio Díaz was another powerful Mexican leader, a great soldier who became president of Mexico. He established a strong centralized government, which he dominated for more than 30 years.

Born into a hard-working *mestizo* family in Oaxaca, Díaz did not have any easy childhood. Like Benito Juárez, he studied first for the priesthood and

imprisoned by President Díaz during the election and lost. While in prison, he came up with the Plan of San Luis Potosí. Madero's plan declared that the election was a fraud and that he would act as president until new elections. The plan also called for an uprising, but Díaz suppressed the revolutionary agitators.

In spite of Díaz's actions, the Revolution began anyway, forcing Díaz to resign. Although Madero was the leader, he couldn't control the various *radical* and conservative components of the Revolution. His ideas were too moderate for both sides. In 1912, Madero was forced to resign at the hands of his own military leaders, and was fatally shot 10 days later while he was being transported to prison.

Lázaro Cárdenas was president of Mexico from 1934 to 1940. He is best known for trying to carry out the goals of the Revolution. Born in Michoacán to a middle-class family, he joined Zapata's rebel army at the age of 18. By 25, he was a general for the government's forces fighting against Zapata. Then he supported the revolt against President Venustiano Carranza, because he thought that Carranza's government was corrupt and not interested in furthering the goals of the Revolution.

After gaining political experience as a governor and leader of his political party, Cárdenas became president. Unlike Madero, he had the support of radical groups, those people who had been most critical of the government during the Revolution and afterward. They trusted him because of his *progressive* views and because he was known for being honest and sincere.

Cárdenas had a Six-Year Plan, which restored much of the power to labor unions, united peasant organizations, redistributed over 40 million acres of land, and created a credit union for those working on *ejidos* (communal farms). Also, he nationalized the petroleum industry, which upset foreign petroleum owners in the

United States and Britain. Finally, he vigorously promoted tourism, celebrating Mexico's rich heritage. Cárdenas remained a presence in Mexican politics until his death in 1970.

For more than 70 years, the Party of the Institutionalized Revolution (PRI) dominated politics in Mexico. In 2000, Mexican businessman Vicente Fox became the first non-PRI candidate elected president of the country since the end of the Mexican Revolution. Before going into politics, Fox had been an executive with Coca-Cola and an independent rancher. He joined the conservative National Action Party (PAN) in 1988, and served as governor of Guanajuato from 1994 to 1999.

As president, Fox's main goals were to improve the educational system, increase political accountability, and allow business and industry to expand the economy with less government interference. The economy did grow during his tenure, although the rate of growth was slow. Fox also attempted to reform the tax system and reduce Mexico's public debt. He also focused

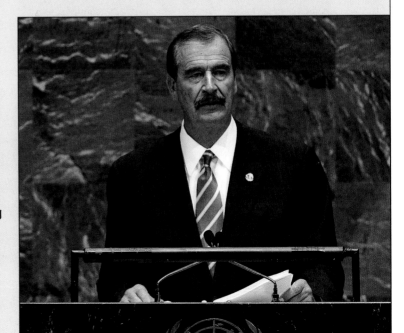

Vicente Fox served as president of Mexico from 2000 to 2006. During his administration, the Mexican economy did not grow as quickly as he had hoped. Still, under Fox, the country's governmental accountability and standard of living improved in many ways.

more on foreign relations than previous presidents had, and urged the United States to implement broad immigration reforms.

Whether or not they agreed with Fox's views, most Mexicans considered the election of a PAN candidate to be a sign that Mexico was becoming a more democratic country, one that was no longer dominated by one political party. After midterm elections in 2003, no party captured a majority of representatives, suggesting that the multi-party system had the potential to last.

In 2006, Felipe Calderón, also a member of PAN, succeeded Fox as president after a very close election. Although the results were controversial and required recounts, the peaceful transfer of power was a positive sign that Mexico was making the transition to a more fair and representative democracy.

Calderón implemented some policies intended to help poorer Mexicans,

Mexican president Enrique Peña Nieto (right) speaks with UN Secretary-General Ban Ki-Moon at an April 2014 seminar in Mexico City.

including caps on the price of staple foods like tortillas, and expanding the education and public health systems. He also encouraged investment in the business sector and expanded free trade agreements with other countries, and as a result Mexico's economy continued to grow during his term.

Felipe Calderón

One of Calderón's more controversial policies was his increased use of federal police and soldiers in a crackdown on Mexican cartels that smuggle drugs into the United States. This "drug war" began in 2006, and quickly became a brutal campaign, with more than 100,000 people killed since then. Although Calderón left office in 2012, his successor, Enrique Peña Nieto, has pledged to continue waging the war against the drug cartels.

TEXT-DEPENDENT QUESTIONS

What Mexican leader served as president from 1934 to 1940?

In 2000, who became the first non-PRI candidate elected president in more than 70 years?

RESEARCH PROJECT

A constitution is a collection of fundamental principles or guidelines that are used to govern a state. Mexico's current constitution was ratified in 1917. Find the Mexican constitution online (the text is available at http://www.juridicas.unam.mx/infjur/leg/constmex/pdf/con-sting.pdf) and read through it. What are some of the rights that the constitution promises to all Mexicans?

 WORDS TO UNDERSTAND

anarchist—one who rebels against all forms of government.

cabinet—an advisory council for a country's leader.

satire—sarcastic humor that often makes fun of social problems and those in power.

A pedestrian walks past the enormous sculpted heads of three 19th-century Mexican patriots—Benito Juárez, Miguel Hidalgo y Costilla, and Venustiano Carranza—in Ensenada, Baja California.

MEXICO'S GREAT THINKERS AND INTELLECTUALS

Many citizens who were not politicians or soldiers shaped the destiny of Mexico. One such Mexican was José Joaquín Fernández de Lizardi, who is remembered as a leading figure of the movement to liberate Mexico from Spain during the early 19th century. He was a novelist, a journalist, and a political activist at a time when Mexico was defining itself as an independent nation.

Lizardi (1776–1827) was born in Mexico City and began studying theology when he was 17. But, like many other famous Mexicans, he chose to go into government service instead of becoming a priest. When the struggle for independence began in 1810, he was a judge in Acapulco. He left politics to start a newspaper called *El Pensador Mexicano* (*The Mexican Thinker*). In his writing, he used **satire** to promote change, but his ideas often made him end up in prison.

When he was imprisoned for writing about his views, he wrote what is considered Mexico's first novel, the title of which is translated as *The Itching Parrot* (1816). Lizardi believed that reading and writing were important forces

39

that could help Mexico become an independent republic, so he founded the Public Society of Reading in 1820, which distributed books and newspapers. Lizardi's contribution to the intellectual life of Mexico encouraged the fight for independence and the creation of the new Mexican nation in the early 19th century.

José Vasconcelos (1882–1959) was a Mexican writer, educator, and philosopher who had a great influence on the development of modern Mexico. He supported the Mexican Revolution that began in 1910, and served as education minister in the government for several years. He believed that education was necessary for freedom, and tried to increase the national literacy rate and provide greater educational opportunities for all Mexicans.

In 1925, Vasconcelos published an essay titled "La raza cósmica" ("The Cosmic Race"), in which he proposed a theory that modern Mexico should blend the most positive characteristics of the country's pre-Colombian past with the best attributes of its Spanish heritage. The resulting *mestizo* civilization would

produce a powerful new race of people, and usher in a great era for humankind, he believed. Vasconcelos's ideas theory became very popular. It was incorporated into the educational system, and influenced the Mexican government's social and economic policies for decades. His writings also influenced and were reflected in the work of Mexican artists like Diego Rivera and Octavio Paz.

Another intellectual who influenced the politics of

José Vasconcelos served several terms as the head of the Mexican government's educational bureau.

Mexican anarchist and social activist Ricardo Flores Magón during the Mexican Revolution against dictator Porfirio Diaz.

Mexico in the early 20th century was Ricardo Flores Magón (1874–1922), a radical thinker whose ideas helped to bring about the Mexican Revolution of 1910. Magón began his life as a radical in 1890, when he was imprisoned for following a student protest against Díaz's government. In 1900, with his brothers, he started *Regeneración (Regeneration)*, an opposition newspaper, which criticized Díaz for bringing progress to Mexico at too high a cost to workers and farm laborers. Together, the Magón brothers began what were called "Liberal Clubs," **anarchist** groups that inspired the ideas of the Revolution, especially ideas about the rights of workers and peasants.

After being imprisoned several times, the Magón brothers went to the United States, where they published *Regeneración* and sent it to workers in Mexico. By 1906, even though it was too dangerous for him to live in Mexico, Ricardo Magón became the leader of a new political party, the Liberal Mexican Party (PLM).

Magón's radical ideas made him many enemies in Mexico and the United States. In 1907, President Díaz persuaded the U.S. government to arrest Magón for encouraging workers to go on strike in Mexican factories. After being imprisoned in the United States several times, Magón was finally charged with espionage and sentenced to 20 years in jail. He died in a Kansas prison in 1916.

Not all great Mexican intellectuals were interested in revolution, however. Alfonso Reyes (1889–1959) was a writer, educator, and diplomat. He began his career writing sophisticated literary criticism while he was still a student. But rather than become a teacher, he went on to receive a law degree. Reyes stayed away from Mexico during the chaotic years that followed the Revolution. Beginning in 1913, he worked for the government as a diplomat, first in Europe, then in Latin America. During his diplomatic career, he continued to write scholarly work but also produced creative pieces, including poetry. As a scholar, he specialized in classical Greek literature and Spanish literature. His creative writing did not reflect the passionate politics of Mexico, but it was still widely respected.

When he retired as a diplomat, Reyes devoted himself to education and scholarship until the end of his career. Under President Cárdenas, he was the director of the *Casa de España*, a school for refugees of the Spanish Civil War. This school later became a famous school of higher education, *El Colegio de México*.

A man of many talents, Agustín Yáñez (1904–1980) had a career similar to his predecessor, Alfonso Reyes. He began his career as a scholar and diplomat, but he became more actively involved in politics than Reyes ever did. However, Yáñez is remembered more for his work as a writer and journalist than as a statesman and politician.

Yáñez's gifts as a student emerged early, and he began teaching when he was only 15, soon becoming a professor at the National University. He began his political career as a diplomat, then became involved in local politics and served as governor of the state of Jalisco from 1953 to 1959.

The most challenging time of Yáñez's political career occurred in 1968, when he was secretary of education in the **cabinet** of President Gustavo Díaz Ordaz. During the late 1960s, Mexico, like much of Europe and the United States, experienced the turmoil and passion of a student movement. Young people publicly demonstrated to show their dissatisfaction with their leaders. In 1968, police and government soldiers fired on a crowd of student protesters at Tlatelolco Plaza in Mexico City, killing many of them and creating a huge crisis. As secretary of education, Yáñez was important in starting a dialogue between the leaders of the student movement and the government. This dialogue prevented further violence.

Alfonso García Robles

In addition to his career in politics, Yáñez worked steadily as a writer. He edited three journals and wrote two well-known novels, *Al Filo del Agua (The Edge of the Storm)* in 1947 and *Las Tierras Flacas (The Lean Lands)* in 1963.

Alfonso García Robles (1911–1991) was another Mexican diplomat and politician who had an enormous impact on international affairs. He helped to establish the United Nations in 1945, and later helped to negotiate the 1967 Treaty of Tlatelolco, in which Latin American countries agreed not to develop or possess nuclear weapons. Robles later represented Mexico at the UN for many years. For his work on nuclear disarmament, he shared the 1982 Nobel Peace Prize with Swedish diplomat Alva Myrdal.

TEXT-DEPENDENT QUESTIONS

What Mexican educator wrote the essay "La raza cósmica" in 1925?

What was the name of the radical magazine published by the Magón brothers?

RESEARCH PROJECT

Imagine that you are a national director of education, like José Vasconcelos or Agustín Yáñez. What are some things that you would change about your school? Explain how these changes would lead to a better educational experience for students.

43

ARTISTS AND WRITERS

Many creative Mexicans contributed to the identity of Mexico through their work. The previous chapter discussed several writers whose ideas shaped Mexico. In this chapter, each artist or writer contributed not only to the shape of Mexican culture but also to the creative field in which he worked.

Manuel Gutiérrez Nájera is an important Mexican poet. He is given credit for connecting Mexican literature to the international ideas of **Modernism**. As a poet, Gutiérrez Nájera attempted to give new life to the language of Spanish poetry and abandoned older Mexican forms in favor of new ideas that came from France. Like other Modernists, Gutiérrez Nájera wanted his writing to express the loneliness and isolation of modern urban life, and his poetry was elegant and somber. While some critics thought that Gutiérrez Nájera's work wasn't Mexican enough, others considered him one of the best of Mexico's poets.

In addition to writing poetry, Gutiérrez Nájera encouraged the work of other poets in his literary journal, *Revista Azul (Blue Review)*, which published the poetry of many young Mexican writers. Sadly, Gutiérrez Nájera died from complications of alcoholism at the age of 36.

One of the most famous figures in Mexico's history is Diego Rivera, a painter

46

who revived the art of large-scale *murals* and who had a huge impact on the international art world. Rivera began his life as an artist at Mexico's Academy of Fine Arts, where he studied from 1898 to 1906. With a government fellowship, he then studied art in Europe, where he was especially fascinated by the frescoes of Renaissance Italy. Rivera lived in Paris and was friends with many great painters, including Pablo Picasso and Henri Matisse. Their new ways of painting and seeing the world had a great influence on him.

Although Rivera was in Europe during the years of the Mexican Revolution, his work was motivated by political ideas. He wanted to bring public art to all the people, not just those who could afford to buy it. Because he was interested in Mexico's native heritage, he combined modern European styles with themes from Mexican history, both ancient and modern.

In the 1930s, Rivera, along with José Clemente Orozco and David Alfaro Siqueiros, started creating murals, putting their large-scale paintings on the walls of public buildings. Rivera's first project was at the National Preparatory School, where his murals created controversy with their political subjects. Not everyone was interested in public art that spoke out against oppression and represented Mexico's native heritage.

Rivera had a passionate personality. Conflict was part of his life as an artist as well as his personal life. He was married several times, twice to Frida Kahlo, who was also a famous artist.

Like Rivera, Octavio Paz (1914–1998) was fascinated by his country's history and by the struggles of its common people. Paz, however, was not a painter but an important

Frescoes are a kind of large-scale painting in which the artist paints on the wet plaster of a wall instead of a canvas. The ceiling of the Sistine Chapel in Rome is covered with the frescoes of Michelangelo, the Renaissance artist.

Mexican writer who won a Nobel Prize in 1990. His work, with its focus on identity issues in a complex and often conflicted culture, has influenced contemporary Latin American writing.

Paz was born in Mexico City in 1914 into a family that cared about books and ideas. His father was a lawyer who had supported Zapata during the Revolution, and his grandfather had an unusually large library, which Paz read as a child. After studying in Mexico, he went to the United States to study Hispanic poetry.

Paz traveled as a writer, going to Spain during the

Octavio Paz (left) received the Nobel Prize for Literature in 1990; to date, he is the only Mexican writer to receive this prestigious award.

Spanish Civil War and, in 1944, to New York to study Spanish American poetry. In 1945, he became a diplomat, serving at posts in Europe, Japan, and India. In 1968, when he heard about the massacre of the student protesters in Tlatelolco Plaza, he resigned his post. He compared the terrible event to the Aztec ritual sacrifices in which those in power used violence to keep order.

48

Not only a novelist but also a political analyst of sorts, Carlos Fuentes has written both about the Mexican and American government systems. Although he has spent much of his life in Mexico, he was raised in Washington, D.C., and visits the United States often.

In his most famous book, *The Labyrinth of Solitude* (1950), Paz analyzed what it means to be Mexican. As in much of his other work, he explored Mexican history and its influence on the Mexican way of thinking. Throughout his life and work, Paz opposed injustice and the violations of human rights.

Another internationally known Mexican writer was Carlos Fuentes (1928–2012), a novelist, playwright, and essayist whose experimental style brought him critical praise. Like Paz, much of Fuentes's writing focused on the connections between the individual Mexican and the complex history of Mexico.

Perhaps the question of what it means to be Mexican was important to Fuentes because he spent the early part of his life outside of Mexico. His father was a diplomat, so he was born in Panama and lived in many other countries before his family returned to Mexico when he was 16.

Fuentes became a diplomat in the 1950s, after receiving a law degree from Mexico's National Autonomous University. From that time on, Fuentes balanced parallel careers in writing and government service. In the 1950s, he started a literary magazine, and he worked as the director of international cultural relations. Like Paz, Fuentes spoke out against the Tlatelolco student massacre in 1968.

Of his more than 20 novels, one of the best known is *The Death of Artemio Cruz* (1962), which follows the life of one man but really is about how Mexico never achieved the goals of the Revolution. Some of his other works include *The Old Gringo* (1985) and *Christopher Unborn* (1987). Fuentes received many important awards for his literary work, and his works have been translated into many languages. When he died in 2012, the *New York Times* called him "one of the most admired writers in the Spanish-speaking world."

 TEXT-DEPENDENT QUESTIONS

In addition to Diego Rivera, which two Mexican artists became known for their murals during the 1930s?

What prestigious literary award did Octavio Paz receive in 1990?

 RESEARCH PROJECT

Diego Rivera and other Mexican muralists of the 20th century were inspired by social and historical events. Ask students to look through the newspaper and find a story that interests them. Then, imagine the people described in the article: are they old or you? Happy or sad? What does their environment look like? On a large (11x17 or 12x18) piece of drawing paper, use crayons or markers to draw a scene related to the newspaper story. Include details that dramatically tell the story.

Xaltelolco.

La Malinche (also known as Doña Marina) interprets for Cortés during a meeting with Aztec emissaries. A former slave who was given to Cortés by one of the tribes he encountered in Mexico, she was an important part of the Spanish success in conquering the Aztecs.

Mexico's Extraordinary Women

For her role in Cortés's conquest of Mexico, La Malinche is considered by some to be an example of a courageous intelligent woman and by others to be a traitor who betrayed her native people to the Spanish conquerors. The daughter of a native nobleman, she had been traded as a slave to another tribe. When Cortés came upon this tribe, she was given to him as a gift and was named Doña Marina. Because she could speak both Mayan and Nahuatl (the language of the Aztecs), she became Cortés's interpreter and companion.

Doña Marina (c. 1496–1529) was from a tribe that had been oppressed by the Aztecs, which may be why she was willing to help the Spaniards with their conquest. She was more than an interpreter, for she gave advice to both Cortés and each Indian community they encountered, helping the native people decide whether to fight Cortés or join him. Her intelligence saved Cortés and his men from several dangerous situations, and she demonstrated her courage by risking her life alongside his soldiers.

Eventually, Doña Marina had a son with Cortés, who was named Martín, after Cortés's father. Before

Nahuatl is still spoken by over one million Mexicans.

52

Cortés left Mexico permanently, he granted her land near the conquered Aztec city of Tenochtitlán, where she established a home with her children and husband, another Spanish soldier.

One of the greatest poets and thinkers of colonial Mexico was also a woman, Sor Juana Inés de la Cruz (1651–1695). She was born in a village outside Mexico City, the illegitimate child of a Basque captain and a *criollo* woman. As a precocious child, she wrote her first poem at the age of eight and could read and write Latin. Her extraordinary intellect impressed the nobles in the court of the Spanish viceroy, Mexico's ruler. She joined the Convent of St. Jerome as a teenager in order to devote herself to an intellectual life, something she felt she could not do if she were to marry.

As a nun, Sor Juana wrote plays, essays, and poetry, and she had a famous large library of 4,000 books. The subject of her writing was often the position and treatment of women. Sor Juana was criticized for wanting to do more than study religious topics. When she was 42, she gave up all her work except her religious studies and sold her books. She died soon afterward during an **epidemic**.

 Here is a translation of one of Sor Juana's poems about the unfairness of men towards women.

Stupid men, quick to condemn
Women wrongly for their flaws,
Never seeing you're the cause
Of all that you blame in them!

Unlike Sor Juana, Empress Carlota (1840–1927) was not truly a Mexican woman but a Belgian princess who became the wife of Emperor Maximilian. A strong personality, she was considered the power behind the throne. Maximilian and Carlota came to Mexico in 1864 as part of the plot of conservative Mexicans and Emperor Napoleon of France. The conservatives thought that they could control Maximilian to

Sor Juana Inés de la Cruz is one of the most recognized historical figures in Mexico. Her striking literary assertions about gender roles and misconceptions are as pointed and challenging today as they were in the 17th century.

regain their power, and meanwhile, Napoleon hoped to have a foothold for his French empire. However, Maximilian didn't do what the conservative Mexicans wanted. Instead, with the support and encouragement of Carlota, he tried to improve conditions in Mexico.

As an outsider in Mexico, Maximilian needed the backing of Napoleon. After the end of the American Civil War, Napoleon foresaw problems with the United States, who didn't want French imperial interests so close to their borders. He withdrew support from Maximilian.

In 1866, Carlota predicted disaster for her husband, so she went to Europe to beg for assistance. After Napoleon refused to keep his original promises to

54

Empress Carlota of Mexico was actually a Belgian princess. She married the Archduke of Austria, who became emperor of Mexico in 1864, but their reign would last only a few years. She spent the last years of her life being treated for mental illness.

support Maximilian, she wrote to her husband that Napoleon was "quite the devil in person." Carlota did not succeed in her quest for help. On her way to ask for the Pope's help in Rome, she showed the first signs of mental illness. She was taken to Belgium, where she lived out the remainder of her life insane, never knowing that her husband had been executed by Juárez's forces.

Not all women involved in Mexican politics did so at their husbands' sides. Brave and independent, Juana Belén Gutiérrez de Mendoza (1875–1942) was a political writer and activist who spoke for the common people during the Mexican Revolution.

Born into a hard-working family in Durango in 1880, she joined the critics of Porfirio Díaz when she was only 21. Although her first published writing was a book of poetry, her most influential work was what she wrote for the newspaper she helped to found. In her newspaper writing, she not only criticized the government but also called on the Mexican people to be more courageous in opposing Díaz.

In 1904, Gutiérrez de Mendoza's passionate writing landed her in prison, where she stayed for three years. When she was released, she joined the followers of Zapata, in the hopes of creating a democratic Mexico. Even after Zapata's death and the disappointments of the government that followed the Revolution, Gutiérrez de Mendoza continued to write about and work for her democratic ideals.

A different type of artist, Frida Kahlo (1907–1954) was a painter whose colorful and highly personal style of painting brought her international fame. The daughter of a German Jewish photographer and his Mexican wife, Kahlo was one of the first women to attend the National Preparatory School.

After a traffic accident in 1924 that fractured her pelvis and shattered her right leg and foot, Kahlo left school and took up painting. She met the muralist Diego Rivera, who recognized her talent and encouraged her work. In 1929, Kahlo married Rivera.

Kahlo found the subjects for her work in her life. Her paintings often focused on her relationship to Rivera and her lifelong pain as a result of the accident. Even so, her identity as a Mexican was essential to her work, and her paintings have many references to Mexico's history and native cultures.

Frida Kahlo's unique artistic vision of her world and herself was fostered by her experiences in Mexico, her relationship with Diego Rivera, and her, at times intense, physical pain due to an accident. Much of her artwork expresses her tormented mental state.

In 2012, Josefina Vázquez Mota became the first woman to run for president of Mexico as the candidate of a major political party, when she was nomination by the National Action Party (PAN). A businesswoman and trained economist, she had been a member of the national legislature and had also been the first woman to serve in two cabinet-level positions in the Mexican government: as minister of the Secretariat of Social Development from 2000 to 2006, and as minister of the

 Because the subject of her work was often strange or dreamlike, art critics labeled Frida Kahlo as a Surrealist, which meant that her work was about the subconscious mind or dreams. Kahlo disagreed. She said: "They thought I was a Surrealist but I wasn't. I never painted dreams. I painted my reality."

57

Secretariat of Public Education from 2006 to 2009. She had also served as a campaign advisor to President Felipe Calderón before deciding to run for the presidency herself in 2012.

These women, from La Malinche to Vázquez, like other famous Mexicans, used their strong personalities and rich heritage to help build a better Mexico.

 ## TEXT-DEPENDENT QUESTIONS
What Mexican activist opposed the government of Porfirio Diaz in the early 20th century? Who was the first Mexican woman to run for president with the support of a major party?

 ## RESEARCH PROJECT
Frida Kahlo is best known for her self-portraits; the artist once explained, "I paint myself because I am so often alone and because I am the subject I know best." Of her 140 paintings known to exist, 55 are self-portraits. Create your own self-portrait using paints, markers, or crayons. Remember that your expression, as well as the clothes or other items you are wearing, and even the background can be used to express emotions or feelings you wish the portrait to convey.

SERIES GLOSSARY

adobe—a building material made of mud and straw.

Amerindian—a term for the indigenous peoples of North and South America before the arrival of Europeans in the late 15th century.

conquistador—any one of the Spanish leaders of the conquest of the Americas in the 1500s.

criollo—a resident of New Spain who was born in North America to parents of Spanish ancestry. In the social order of New Spain, criollos ranked above mestizos.

fiesta—a Mexican party or celebration.

haciendas—large Mexican ranches.

maquiladoras—factories created to attract foreign business to Mexico by allowing them to do business cheaply.

mariachi—a Mexican street band that performs a distinctive type of music utilizing guitars, violins, and trumpets.

Mesoamerica—the region of southern North America that was inhabited before the arrival of the Spaniards.

mestizo—a person of mixed Amerindian and European (typically Spanish) descent.

Nahuatl—the ancient language spoken by the Aztecs; still spoken by many modern Mexicans.

New Spain—name for the Spanish colony that included modern-day Mexico. This vast area of North America was conquered by Spain in the 1500s and ruled by the Spanish until 1821.

plaza—the central open square at the center of Spanish cities in Mexico.

pre-Columbian—referring to a time before the 1490s, when Christopher Columbus landed in the Americas.

FURTHER READING

Foster, Lynn V. *A Brief History of Mexico*. New York: Checkmark Books, 2007.

Fowler, Will. *Santa Anna of Mexico*. Lincoln: University of Nebraska Press, 2007.

Fox, Vicente. *Revolution of Hope: The Life, Faith, and Dreams of a Mexican President*. New York: Plume, 2008.

Gritzner, Charles F. *Mexico*. New York: Chelsea House, 2012.

Herrera, Hayden, et al. *Frida Kahlo*. Minneapolis: Walker Art Center, 2007.

Kent, Deborah. *Mexico*. New York: Children's Press, 2012.

Levy, Buddy. *Conquistador: Hernán Cortés, King Montezuma, and the Last Stand of the Aztecs*. New York: Bantam, 2008.

Lozano, Luis Martin, and Juan Coronel Rivera. *Diego Rivera: The Complete Murals*. New York: Taschen, 2008.

Reef, Catherine. *Frida & Diego: Art, Love, Life*. New York: Clarion Books, 2014.

Williams, Colleen Madonna Flood. *The People of Mexico*. Philadelphia: Mason Crest, 2015.

Pancho Villa, surrounded by members of his army, stands with his hand on the barrel of an artillery piece, circa 1915.

INTERNET RESOURCES

Sor Juana Inés de la Cruz Project
http://www.dartmouth.edu/~sorjuana

The Virtual Diego Rivera Museum
http://www.diegorivera.com

Mesoweb
http://www.mesoweb.com/welcome.html#externalresources

History of Mexico
http://www.history.com/topics/mexico

Frida Kahlo and Diego Rivera are two of Mexico's most famous artists.

INDEX

63

PICTURE CREDITS

ABOUT THE AUTHOR

Anna Carew-Miller is a freelance writer and former teacher. She lives in rural Connecticut with her husband, her daughter, and a very large cat. They enjoy hiking, backpacking, and cross-country skiing. Anna has a B.A. in English from the College of William and Mary, an M.A. in English from Yale University, and a Ph.D. in American Literature from the University of New Mexico. She has done extensive research and writing on women in literature, nature writing, and Native American literature.